Original title:
Tides of the Forgotten

Copyright © 2025 Creative Arts Management OÜ
All rights reserved.

Author: Ryan Sterling
ISBN HARDBACK: 978-1-80587-430-0
ISBN PAPERBACK: 978-1-80587-900-8

Haunting of the Forgotten Waters

In a world where fish wear hats,
And mermaids juggle with their spats,
Ghostly crabs dance on the shore,
While seaweed sings, "Give me more!"

Old boots float by, full of dreams,
Whispers of giants with ice cream beams,
A pirate sneezes, swabs the deck,
Chasing seagulls with a bag of peck!

Bubbles giggle, tickling toes,
While lobsters play hide and seek in rows,
A whale jokes (oh, what a sight!),
Knocking over boats, laughing with delight!

So splash through these waters, a laugh or two,
Where every wave brings a silly view,
In the depths of fun, we forget our woes,
As we dance with fishes, where the humor flows!

Driftwood Stories Untold

Once a log danced with a crab,
Claiming the title of king to grab.
Said the sea, "You're a bit out of line,"
"Your crown is merely a seaweed twine!"

The barnacles laughed, gave a cheer,
Sung of adventures, both far and near.
Each tide brought tales, absurd and wild,
Of whales who rhymed, just like a child!

Faded Footprints by the Water's Edge

Old footprints vanish, just like socks,
The ocean steals them, oh what a fox!
With every wave, a dancer's trace,
A shuffle of shoes in a funny race.

Toe prints argue, left and right,
"Which way to go?" they laugh in fright.
Seagulls hoot and mock the fun,
As they steal snacks from everyone!

Beneath the Surface of Remembered Things

Fish gossip under bubbles of soap,
Chatting of crabs who read the horoscope.
"I'll find love, just wait for the moon,"
Said a flounder, who hummed a tune.

Starfish twirl, feeling quite proud,
In their own little world, they're not cowed.
"Who needs legs when you can just cling?"
Said one as he practiced his salsa swing!

Surging Silence of the Deep

Down below, the fish wear hats,
In pockets, they craft binding contracts.
"Let's start a band!" a clownfish proposed,
While a squid juggled pearls, slightly dozed.

An octopus writes, with ink on a shell,
Stories of shenanigans, oh what a swell!
They'll laugh and they'll giggle, beneath the tide,
In the great underwater, where secrets reside!

Whispers of Abandoned Shores

Seagulls squawk with a silly glee,
Chasing crabs as they dance by the sea.
Old driftwood tells tales of lost flip-flops,
While starfish giggle on the kelpy tops.

Sandcastles rise, then tumble down fast,
With moats that are filled with water from the past.
Children's laughter floats in the air,
While seashells whisper secrets to a nearby chair.

Echoes in the Sand

Footprints meander, then vanish so quick,
Like socks in the laundry, they played a cruel trick.
Beach balls bounce like they're high on caffeine,
While sand flies like confetti, causing a scene.

A crab, in its armor, dances a jig,
It's the king of the beach, but it's really quite big.
Surfboards slide, but mostly they fall,
An awkward ballet, the beach's own ball.

Lost Currents of Time

Time slips away like a fish out of net,
Reminding us all not to place any bet.
Old flip-flops linger, they won't take a ride,
While umbrellas dance as the breezes collide.

Sunscreen's a slippery, sticky old friend,
It's really no wonder, we lose it again.
With seagulls above, making mischief at play,
Who knew a vacation could go so astray?

Shadows Beneath the Waves

Beneath the waves, where the sea cucumbers roam,
A party is starting, but no one's at home.
Lobsters wear hats, and they're ready to dance,
While octopuses juggle, giving fish a chance.

Anemones sway with whimsical grace,
While turtles spin tales in this curious place.
The sea is alive, with giggles and fun,
While we sunbathe above, soaked in warm sun.

Driftwood Tales of the Unseen

A stick floats by, don't let it go,
It's telling stories of friends below.
With each wave laugh, it's all a game,
Old shoes and socks, they have no shame.

Seaweed twists like a dancing cat,
It tickles fish, and runs off flat.
The king crab wears a crown made of shells,
While clams whisper secrets between their bells.

A turtle grins, with wise old eyes,
He winks and says, "It's a crazy prize!"
Seagulls gossip, they cackle so bright,
Over driftwood tales in the shining light.

So come and sit by this wavy shore,
Grab a driftwood stick, let's tell some more.
The unseen laughs in the salty air,
Embrace the nonsense, if you dare!

The Undercurrent of Lost Voices

The murmurs bubble beneath the tide,
Fish gossip tales, with nowhere to hide.
A clam's a poet, with verses to share,
He hums a tune without a care.

A jellyfish floats, all dressed in glitz,
Spreading sweet rumors, she never sits.
In this ballroom of bubbles, they dance away,
Spinning tales of the silliest play.

Every foot that trips on sandy rumbles,
Echoes of laughter as the ocean fumbles.
Old pirates tease with their ghostly charms,
While crabs do the cha-cha, raising their arms.

So dive down deep, lose your frowns,
Join the frolic in the undersea towns.
For when the sirens laugh and tease,
You'll find joy in the waves and breeze.

Forgotten Harbors of the Heart

In a harbor where socks lost their mates,
Lurks a fish who picks up the fates.
He tells of sailors and their blunders,
While seagulls squawk, rolling their wonders.

Old boats sway, they whisper and sigh,
Dreaming of distances, they want to fly.
A rubber duck floats, proud of its fame,
While rusty anchors play guess the name.

In the corners, old anchors hold grudge,
Counting each wave with an ever-so-slight sludge.
The laughter rolls, as waves collide,
Nautical friends play hide and seek with pride.

So gather round for a nautical laugh,
The harbors of hearts tell you the path.
Embrace the quirks of ocean's delight,
As shells serenade you into the night!

Sunken Echoes from Another Time

Bubbles rise with a giggling sound,
As sunken treasures spin round and round.
A goldfish king with a crown of seaweed,
Commands the clams in their undersea feed.

An old clock ticks, but the time's all wrong,
Winding up tales for a mermaid's song.
The bass drum thumps from an oyster shell,
Spreading the gossip where the eels all dwell.

Waves crash laughter on a sandy bed,
Where mermaids dance with jellyfish spread.
Sea cucumbers moan, a grumpy old crew,
While barnacles pipe up, singing "Woo-hoo!"

So dive into secrets, where bubbles hold rhyme,
For the echoes of laughter transcend the time.
In sunken splendor, let joy be your guide,
And revel in stories the tides try to hide!

The Sorrowful Song of the Current

The fish all gathered for a feast,
They played their tunes, not very beast.
The bubbles rose with every note,
While crabs just danced and tried to float.

A seaweed band struck up a cheer,
The jellies swayed, they showed no fear.
But when a shark came for a snack,
The music died, no time to snack!

They gurgled songs of lost delight,
As waves crashed hard and filled with fright.
Yet every tune began with glee,
Until that shark cried, "Don't eat me!"

And so they laughed through all their plight,
In currents deep, they found their light.
With every wave, they sang anew,
The fish still laughed, and that's not blue!

Obscured Echoes Beneath the Moon

Beneath the moon, the shadows play,
With clams that gossip night and day.
The oysters chuckle in their beds,
While lobsters weave tales in their heads.

A crab with jokes, oh what a sight,
He balances pearls, a comical fright.
"Why did the fish blush?" they all ask,
"Because he saw the shellfish bask!"

The tides gave whispers, soft and slight,
As minnows twirled in silly flight.
The moonlit dance was quite absurd,
As sea stars giggled, not a word!

In waters deep, the laughter grew,
It echoed wide, each rippling hue.
As night rolled on, the fun would swell,
With underwater jokes, all went well!

Fragments of the Drowned Past

In the depths, where treasures lie,
A lost sock met an old fish's eye.
"Who wears such things?" the fish did sigh,
"Not me, I swim, not dry and shy!"

A sunken boot with tales to tell,
Of parties held where crabs do dwell.
The barnacles sang a funny tune,
As bubbles laughed beneath the moon.

A sailor's hat drifted by with flair,
The jellyfish wore it, without a care.
"It's quite a look!" they all agreed,
"A stylish hat indeed, oh heed!"

The fragments told of days gone by,
In laughs and giggles, not a single cry.
For in the depths of ocean's hold,
Lies humor deep, in legends bold!

The Whispering Breeze of Lost Hope

The breeze blew softly, tickling fins,
As sea cows recited the silliest sins.
"Did you hear what that whale said?"
"He's dreaming of tacos while sleeping in bed!"

A playful dolphin jumped and spun,
"Don't trust the fish who say they run!"
With giggles shared from wave to wave,
The ocean's laughter, all they crave.

They waved goodbye to worries past,
As plankton danced, their fun was vast.
With every swirl, they'd twist and glide,
The ocean's heart, an endless ride.

So if you listen, you might hear,
The whispers of hope, bringing cheer.
In salty breezes, joy is found,
With every chuckle, love's profound!

Drift of Forgotten Echoes

In the sand, I lost my shoe,
And wondered if it once knew,
The secret paths of crabs and clams,
Or if it's just one of my scams.

Seagulls cackle 'bout lost things,
While waves dance, and the sea sings,
A sock floats by, what a sight!
Guess it's a party tonight!

Shells are whispering silly tales,
Of pirate ships with floppy sails,
As the sun sets with a grin,
I'm pretty sure I've gone swim!

Forgotten echoes make a ruckus,
Bubbles giggle, water's chuckus,
In this frothy, comfy spot,
Life's a joke — oh, is it not?

The Coastline of Lost Dreams

I dreamt of gold, but found a broom,
Next to a hat that smelled like gloom,
The sun wakes up, shining bright,
Guess perfection took a flight.

Turtles jog in speedos and hats,
While crabs boogie, shaking their fats,
All the fish are rolling in laughter,
Maybe dreams aren't what we're after.

A coconut rolled by, all alone,
It looked like a terrible phone,
I tried to call my dreams with care,
But all I got was salty air.

So here I sit, lost but glad,
Life's a joke, yet it's not bad,
In the sand, I laugh out loud,
With my mismatched shoes, I'm proud!

Abandoned Ports of Our Lives

Once a ship sailed, now it's a dock,
Where sea monsters play hopscotch and mock,
Nonsense looms in the salty breeze,
As I wave to lost memories with ease.

A buoy wiggles, waving its hands,
It tells me tales of far-off lands,
With legends of mermaids gone mad,
And seagulls that made the sailors sad.

A rusty anchor tries to dance,
Trip on it? Oh, take a chance!
Laughing waves splash as I fall,
Life's a circus, and I'm the call.

So here at the quay, I'll stay a while,
Sharing jokes, crafting my style,
With all the oddities, I've befriended,
In these ports, nothing's ever ended.

The Lullaby of Distant Waters

Bubbles sing a lullaby sweet,
To fish in pajamas, what a treat,
The stars yawn wide, night's in their eyes,
While whispers of seaweed giggle and rise.

A jellyfish with floppy hats,
Tells jokes to snails and chatting rats,
Crabs dance around in a comical trance,
All here waiting for dawn's romance.

Splash! The waves titter and sway,
Tickling toes as they play,
A whale pops up with a splashy grin,
Declaring this revelry will begin!

So come join this watery spree,
With giggling friends under the sea,
In the lullaby of night's soft charms,
We drift in laughter with open arms.

Sea Glass Testimonies of Yore

In the driftwood's laugh, secrets do hide,
Old bottles float by, on the ocean's wide ride.
A message of love, yet a sock in the clay,
Who needs sensitivity when you're lost in the bay?

A fish reports tales of a sailor's grand tale,
Of his epic quest for a fresh seafood sale.
But cannery workers, they sure know the score,
They've seen his kind come, then they publish no more.

With glass so bright, they shine like a flare,
"Hey there!" they shout, "Do we care or not care?"
The legends forget, but the bubbles still sing,
Of jellyfish parties and shellfish bling-bling!

So gather your shards, let's toast and let's cheer,
To memories lost, over salty sea beer.
For in every strange find, laughter may grow,
In the humor of fish tales, there's magic, you know!

Eclipsed Memories Beneath the Waves

Beneath the seafoam, a starfish does pout,
He lost his good friend, but he's still hanging out.
"Where'd you swim off to?" he shouts in despair,
"I can't do this dance while I'm lost in mid-air!"

The snails are just munching on popcorn they find,
While mermaids are giggling, a little unkind.
"Oh dear, look at him, he's stuck on a hook,
Someone play baritone, let's write him a book!"

The crabs start to scuttle, with laughter they flee,
They thump on twin oceans, as wild as can be.
"Did you hear about Flipper, who took a wrong turn?
He's a legend now—with a grin and a burn!"

So twirl with the seaweed, let laughter ignite,
In these waves of the playful, there's humor in sight.
For every lost memory, a giggle accounts,
When echoing laughter in ocean amounts.

Forgotten Lanterns in the Mist

Lanterns swing low, in a fog of surprise,
Casting shadows of squid, with very quick ties.
A light bulb that flickers, oh dear, what a fool,
That fish did not know it was bait for the school!

The barnacles giggle, in their crusted up shells,
As waves tell tall tales of the underwater spells.
But truth be told, it's quite hard to perceive,
When gobies bump heads and they dance to deceive!

A sea turtle's sneer, "What is this nonsense?"
He trips on a rock, "Hey, can I get some sense?"
His friends all roar laughter, as he rolls in the krill,
"Quick, call the fish doc, it's giving me chills!"

While lanterns may falter, and beams may go dim,
The joy of the laugh hides where silliness swims.
So let's bring a tribute, to stories that drift,
For amidst all the dangers, it's humor that's gifted.

Currents of the Forsaken Mind

A dolphin was dreaming, beneath a green wave,
Of marshmallow clouds, which were soft and so brave.
But half of his thoughts, were caught in a net,
He swam round in circles, yet still had no regret!

The jellyfish wobble, with tentacles swayed,
While seahorses giggle, in their little parade.
"Did you see that old clam? He just let out a sigh,
He misses his pearl, but who cares, oh my!"

With thoughts in the whirlpool, ideas take flight,
They dance like a wave, in the glow of the night.
And as eels start debating, about what makes them slime,
They laugh at the current; it's just more fun time!

So let's toast to the ripples, of minds bold and free,
In the ocean of laughter, forever we'll be.
For currents may twist, and our thoughts may unwind,
But we'll always find joy in the depths of the mind!

Remnants of a Distant Echo

Whispers of a laughing wave,
Chasing crumbs from yesterday's crave.
A crab with a juggling flair,
Dropped his shell without a care.

Drifting thoughts play hide-and-seek,
Fish wear hats that look so chic.
Gulls overhead squawk silly jokes,
As barnacles dance with old sea folks.

Bubbles pop with quirky glee,
Shells whisper tales of the deep blue spree.
With porpoises joining in the play,
Echoes of laughter wash the blues away.

Forgotten flotsam on the shore,
Sips of sunlight, wanting more.
With each wave that tumbles near,
Memory's cocktail, served with cheer.

Secrets of the Silent Sea

Beneath the surface, a seaweed tease,
Where turtles plot with jellyfish ease.
Octopus wears his party pants,
Trying to flirt with the fishy dance.

Conch shells hold a gossip ring,
While sea cucumbers try to sing.
A dolphin spins with perfect grace,
While seahorses match his pace.

Clams debate what's in the pot,
With tales of treasure that they've got.
Ghost crabs with their moonlit smiles,
Running races over sandy miles.

A whisper of laughter in the breeze,
Where sea grasses sway with the tease.
What's lost in the murky frame,
Is a party where all are the same.

When Memories Drift Away

Drifting dreams on a foam-topped wave,
Mermaids giggle, misbehave.
With a wink, the sea turtle grins,
"Last I saw, a ship lost its fins!"

The sun yawns, splashing gold around,
Seashells hide under the sandy ground.
Starfish playing hide-and-seek,
While dolphins leap and little fish squeak.

Old stories ride on each gentle swell,
Of barnacles with tales to tell.
Caught in the tide, they twist and twirl,
"Did you know?" they whisper and swirl.

With each splash, laughter flows free,
Recalling an octopus wearing a key.
In this watery realm of the now,
Memories float, taking a bow.

The Lament of Ebbing Waters

Once where laughter filled the air,
Now a fish grumbles in despair.
"Where have all the good times gone?
I swear I saw them swim at dawn!"

The tide pulled back, took joy away,
Leaving shells to play their forlorn play.
A lonely starfish attempts a dance,
Trip over a sandcastle in a trance.

"Maybe they'll come back someday,
With frolicking waves that want to stay."
The seaweed shakes with laughter loud,
A playful spirit breaking the shroud.

Yet the tide keeps ebbing, laughter fades,
As sea otters snicker at the charades.
In murky depths where secrets dwell,
Echoes of giggles weave their spell.

The Shoreline of What Once Was

On sands where slippers used to trot,
A crab dons shades, looking quite hot.
Seagulls gossip, sharing their lunch,
While shells whisper tales of a wild punch.

The beach ball rolls, it's lost its bounce,
While flip-flops dance, they start to prance.
A fish wears a tie, thinking it's grand,
While jellyfish juggle, oh isn't it bland?

Old driftwood sits, a throne for the crabs,
As they toast with sea foam—just little drabs.
The sun winks down with a cheeky grin,
As barnacles laugh at where they've been.

So let's raise a toast to forgotten things,
Where laughter and silliness always sings.
On shores of history, we'll dance with glee,
As the waves nod back in a quirky spree.

Unveiling the Lost Stories of the Sea

In waves so high, a fish recites,
The tale of sailors and their silly fights.
A whale takes notes, scribbling with flair,
While dolphins giggle, flipping in air.

A treasure chest, it's full of socks,
The pirate's nightmare - oh what a paradox!
With rumors of gold, but it's really just fluff,
A show of misplaced and mismatched stuff.

Octopus chefs cook up seaweed stew,
While sea turtles rock out, sporting a shoe.
A starfish DJ spins tales on the reef,
As creatures join in, sharing their grief.

So gather 'round mates for a whimsical chat,
Of lost stories told by a wise old brat.
The sea has secrets, so funny and weird,
Wave after wave, that's how we've steered.

The Ghost of Undesired Silence

In the hush of the deep, where the lost fishes dwell,
A ghost of a clam rings a faint dinner bell.
With echoes of laughter that few ever catch,
A skeleton squid plans an unscripted match.

A whisper floats by, it's a crab with a hat,
"Why don't you call? I'm too scared of that!"
The starfish replies, "I'm stuck here, you see,
But let's fasten some bubbles, just you and me!"

The seaweed sways, with giggles galore,
As whispers of fun slink around to explore.
A fish in a bow tie approaches with glee,
"A party's afoot! Come join our jamboree!"

Yet still echoes linger, as silence might sneak,
When laughter tumbles over, the quirks start to leak.
So let's make the sound of the ocean our guide,
In the land of the forgotten—joy must abide!

Riptides of Memories Unraveled

The waves suck you in, but it's all in good fun,
As memories twist like a dive in the sun.
A hermit crab squawks, "Where's my old home?"
While fish tell tall tales of frolicking foam.

Once a king conch with a throne made of sand,
Now sips lemonade, isn't life just grand?
The barnacles clink, toasting all they've seen,
As memories flop on the bright marine screen.

Octopus dancers whirl with glee,
"Remember last summer? Just you and me?"
They swirl in the ripples, a salty old dream,
As history bubbles, a fizzy ice cream.

So here's to the moments we sometimes forget,
To laughter and joy, we owe them our debt.
In the riptides of time, let's savor each pulse,
As the sea shares its secrets, no need to repulse.

The Ocean's Lament for the Lost

There once was a fish named Fred,
Who lost his way, filled with dread.
He swam in circles, quite forlorn,
Wishing he had maps to adorn.

The octopus chuckled in glee,
"Just follow the bubbles, you see?"
Fred flailed his fins, oh what a sight,
Blinded by sunlight, but oh so bright.

A crab then joined in on the dance,
"Stop sulking, Fred, give life a chance!"
Together they twirled, flipping in glee,
Creating quite the ruckus at sea.

So here's to fish lost and found,
With laughter and joy all around.
Though maps might help keep fear at bay,
Sometimes it's fun to just play all day!

Secrets of the Shimmering Deep

In the depths where the mermaids sing,
They hide a tale of the silliest thing.
A clam named Lou, well, he loved to brag,
About treasures in his shiny rag.

One day a dolphin swam by with a grin,
"Hey Lou, where's the sparkle, I see none within!"
Lou puffed his pearl, boasting away,
Till it popped with a bang, what a day!

The seaweed danced, what a hullabaloo,
As fish gathered round for the show, who knew?
With laughter and bubbles, they couldn't stop,
The clam's big tale, it came to a flop!

Yet Lou was happy, despite the flop,
For laughter and friends, they never could stop.
Secrets of depths, some silly, some grand,
In the shimmering deep, all go hand in hand!

Ebbing Memories of Yesterday

Once in a tidepool lived a wise snail,
Who often told jokes with a long, slimy trail.
"I remember the time I raced with a flea,
His jumps were bold, but I cruised with glee!"

The sea stars laughed as they twinkled so bright,
"Dear snail, you're slow, but your jokes are a delight!"
A crab chimed in, "Tell us one more,
Before the tide comes to wash us ashore!"

The snail puffed out his chest with great pride,
"Why did the seaweed never move aside?
Because it was too 'algae' to shift and sway,
Just like my cousin when rained on all day!"

In the ebbing tides, where the laughter flows,
Memories linger, as everyone knows.
Cherishing moments with jokes so grand,
Yesterday's tales, just hand in hand!

Where the Sea Remembers

In the shallows where the sea meets the shore,
A crab lost a shoe; oh, what a bore!
He searched high and low, from rock to rock,
Only to trip on a giant sea clock.

"Who thought time could be so unkind?"
He grumbled and gripped his head, confined.
A friendly fish winked, "Just tap your feet,
Find the rhythm and dance to the beat!"

With a twist and a shimmy, they danced through the sand,

The crab and his new fishy band.
Laughter erupted from the shells all around,
As the ocean echoed with joy, profound.

Now the crab wears a conch, styled just right,
With seaweed adorned, a glamorous sight!
Where memories linger in laughter and cheer,
The ocean remembers, always so near.

Forgotten Shores at Dusk

On the sandy beach, crabs do dance,
While seagulls squawk, and they're in a trance.
A flip-flop lost, what a sight to see,
It flops alone, longing to be free.

Old chairs reclined, a sunburned plight,
As sunscreen battles with sand's delight.
An ice cream cone melts on the ground,
Laughter echoes, playful sounds abound.

In shadows cast, the beach umbrellas,
Join the party with the drunken jellies.
As waves giggle, they keep their chase,
Seeking the laughter to embrace.

Oh, to be forgotten by the shore,
With flip-flops and sunscreens, who could ask for more?
A toast with seashells, clink them tight,
On these shores, we'll laugh all night!

The Hushed Cries of Castaway Souls

Once upon a log, a man in despair,
Waves whispered jokes; he let out a stare.
A coconut hat on his head did rest,
He looked quite dapper for a castaway guest.

Messages in bottles, a grand old jest,
Sometimes they bring pizza, at worst they're a pest.
With palm trees dancing, they sway in glee,
While crabs play poker, sipping on tea.

A treasure map scribbled in ketchup stains,
The x marks the spot where fun reigns.
"Help!" he shouted, but the tide made it clear,
A bucket of seaweed was all that came near.

Yet laughter echoes through the salt and foam,
His island life turned into a home.
With rumors of dancing sea turtles too,
Dreams of escape brewed with coconut stew!

Mists of the Lost Horizon

In foggy realms where mermaids droll,
The fish wear suits, they're on a stroll.
With bubbles and giggles, they sneak a peek,
At sailors who stumble, too tired to speak.

The compass spins 'round—what a fright!
Guided by starfish shining so bright.
With a wink and a splash, they set sail anew,
For a treasure that's made of seaweed stew.

"Ahoy there, matey!" a dolphin does squeal,
For each fishy tale, there's a juicy meal.
Caught in a net, a crab starts to croon,
He's got a concert under the moon.

Lost in a haze, but laughter's in stock,
Forget all your worries, just let them dock.
In the mists of fun, they live life with flair,
With seaweed hats and nothing to wear!

Celestial Memories Adrift

Stars shine above on this whimsical night,
As jellyfish disco beneath moonlight bright.
With canoes made of laughter, they glide and they sway,
An octopus DJ, spinning beats in the bay.

The sky's full of wishes, and they float like dreams,
While starfish tell stories of odd little schemes.
A comet's a visit, with an ice cream delight,
"More sprinkles!" they shout, "What a glorious sight!"

Forgotten wishes dance on the tide,
In rainbow formations, they choose to reside.
With giggles and whirlwinds, the night starts to hum,
Each wave is a song, inviting the fun.

So here's to the skies, and the seas we adore,
Where every little splash brings a grin and a roar.
With memories adrift, we'll sing to the moon,
For laughter and love, we'll always make room!

Faded Memories in Salt Air

A crab stole my sandwich today,
With a dance that was quite the display.
He scuttled away with a grin,
Leaving me in a state of chagrin.

Seagulls laughed from a nearby pier,
As I pondered my lunch and a beer.
Old flip-flops floated by with a snicker,
Life here moves slow, but dreams come quicker.

Sandy socks tell tales of the past,
Of beach days that went by too fast.
With each tide, I lose more and more,
Will I find my sandwich along the shore?

But laughter rings through this salty breeze,
As I chase after crumbs, if you please.
Who knew that a meal could cause such fuss?
I'll just wave to the crab, he's the real plus.

The Ruins of Distant Dreams

I built a castle, high and grand,
With popsicle sticks and beachy sand.
A wave rolled in, oh what a fright!
My dream home met its watery plight.

My bucket's now a throne for a fish,
Who claims my kingdom as his own wish.
"Your reign is over!" I cry with glee,
"I'll build it higher, just wait and see!"

Seashells whisper notes of the day,
As I scoff at what they might say.
Who needs an empire made of sand,
When I can dance and make my stand?

The laughter of waves as my kingdom falls,
Is enough to erase my silly brawls.
Forgotten dreams washed up on shore,
But I'll create again, oh, I'll make more!

Dreams Adrift on Forgotten Currents

My beach ball floats on a lost quest,
As it dodges the waves, what a jest!
It seems to think it's got a say,
In where it lands on this sunny day.

Flip-flops wearing a tan like a boss,
Gather shells like they're at a loss.
"Hey, buddy, your sole is showing through!"
As crabs hop by with a snicker or two.

Waves tell tales that the sun forgot,
Of beach umbrellas in a tangled knot.
But who needs order in this sand-n-sun?
Life's a party; let's have some fun!

So, if you find my lost beachy dreams,
Just laugh along with my quirky schemes.
As I stand here, with my frosty drink,
Who knew waves could make you think?

Remnants of a Vanished Tide

Once a grand ship, now a memory,
Lost among seashells and glee.
It's captained by a seagull with flair,
Laughing at treasure, just filled with air.

Dunes are the pirates, buried in jest,
Guarding the secrets they love the best.
A map drawn in ketchup, so rare,
Leads to a burger left floating in air.

As waves take my dreams out for a ride,
I wonder if they've got nowhere to hide.
Old surfboards claim they're kings to this land,
While my dreams sell snacks—oh, isn't that grand?

So linger awhile in this salty fun,
As stories unfold beneath the sun.
The sea's full of giggles, clever and sly,
While I chase my cap and let out a sigh.

Melodies from the Deep Blue

A fish in a tux, what a sight!
He dances with shrimp in the pale moonlight.
The octopus claps with eight big hands,
As jellyfish waltz in their glittering bands.

A crab sings a tune with a tiny guitar,
While seahorses round dance in a little bar.
The seaweed grooves to the bubbles' beat,
And starfish cheer from their comfy seat.

A whale tries to rap, but it's quite the mess,
His rhymes are as old as a barnacle's dress.
Dolphins chuckle at his failed routine,
In the deep blue where laughter is seen.

So join in the chorus, let joy abound,
In the salty abyss where silliness is found.
With melodies floating on watery threads,
Let's sing for the fish with the great big heads!

Lost Currents of Memory

Remember that time we swam in a shoe?
With fish doing flips in a bizarre view.
A clam told a joke, but we missed the pun,
Now we just laugh, thinking it was fun.

We chased after bubbles, like puppies on sand,
Hoping to catch what we didn't understand.
Seashells were treasures, but we sold them cheap,
In the grand bazaar where memories leap.

An eel wore a hat, thinking he was grand,
While crabs shuffled sideways, in a conga line band.
We're lost in the waves, with giggles and glee,
Recalling the days of our scallywag spree.

As the memory drifts, like driftwood on shore,
We laugh at the mishaps, still wanting more.
For in the depths, our hearts do embrace,
The currents of laughter that time can't erase.

Silted Sorrows of the Past

Once a mermaid lost her favorite comb,
She searched high and low, far from her home.
A crab found it first, tried it on for size,
Now he's the chicest with sparkly eyes.

Old seaweed whispers of fishes long gone,
As clams tell their stories from dusk until dawn.
But like any drama, it comes with a twist,
As sunken treasures are often just mist.

With pearls in the silt, they plan a parade,
While the pufferfish pouts, feeling dismayed.
A seahorse sighs, as he tidies his hair,
In a world full of memories, light as the air.

So let out a chuckle, don't dwell on the gloom,
For silted sorrows can still make a room.
With laughter in currents and bubbles a-blow,
We dance through the past, letting funny things flow.

Beneath the Moonlit Surface

The surfboards of turtles, they ride with such flair,
While dolphins juggle shells, quite the oceanic fare.
A clownfish cracks jokes as he swims through the kelp,
While a starfish tries stand-up—it's all quite the help!

Beneath moonlit waves, where silliness glows,
The creatures unite in a sponge cake pose.
Anemones giggle, tickled by sea breeze,
As whales hum a tune, making everyone sneeze.

The eels take a bow, all tangled in laughs,
While shrimps do their best in hilarious gaffs.
The night sparkles bright, as the sea comes alive,
In this murky wonder, where humor can thrive.

So dive into joy, let the laughter submerge,
For beneath the moonlight, silliness will surge.
In the whimsical depths, where all the weird plays,
We find that fun resides in the ocean's maze!

The Abyssal Chronicles

In the depths where the fish wear hats,
A clam organizes chatty chitchats.
Octopuses play card games with glee,
While sea cucumbers take naps by the sea.

A crab with a monocle tells a joke,
His punchlines make the dolphins choke.
With shells for seats, they laugh until night,
In this underwater comedy, everything's light.

A starfish spills secrets, oh what a mess,
While jellyfish dance in a sparkly dress.
Between barnacles and stripes of the tide,
In the ocean's own club, there's no place to hide.

Mermaids are rapping, such a wild sound,
As turtles bobbed up, gathering around.
In this abyss, where all laughs collide,
The chronicles of giggles never subside.

Where Sundown Meets the Forgotten

At dusk, the lost fish made a quirky pact,
To all wear sunglasses, just for the act.
A grouper in sneakers tries running the show,
While seahorses giggle and sway to the flow.

A whale blows bubbles, bursting with cheer,
While shrimps do the limbo without any fear.
The sun sets slowly, painting the sea,
In humor and laughter—oh, what a spree!

Frogs from the beach come to see the display,
With frogs in a conga, they hop and sway.
The sardines swirl, showing off their new flair,
While crabs in a conga line dance without care.

In the twilight glow, they spin tales and fables,
Where memories waltz on the shimmering tables.
With each goofy twitch, they banish despair,
A joyous reunion, laughter fills the air.

Castaway Whispers

On a beach made of jelly, the castaways grin,
As they share their tales of mischief and din.
A parrot recites poems of silly delight,
While sandy-faced buddies roleplay all night.

A coconut drinks soda under the sun,
Sipping it slowly, oh, isn't it fun?
With friends by the shore, the world is a jest,
From seaweed to shells, they're surely the best!

A turtle's been boasting of races and speed,
While crabs snap their claws, taking turns to lead.
A conch shell is laughing, it joins in the spree,
As driftwood and sandcastles dance by the sea.

With whispers of laughter floating in air,
Under star-studded skies, they dance without care.
In this playful land, where dreams take their flight,
The castaways shine like stars in the night!

Ghosts of the Ocean Floor

Down below where the seaweed sways,
The ghosts throw parties in laughable ways.
With old pirate tales that stumble and trip,
And fish with the giggles that just cannot quit.

A wobbly jelly, in shadows it glides,
Telling fishy jokes while it hides and it hides.
In the haunt of the shipwreck, with bubbles that burst,
They reminisce about treasure they've lost at the worst.

A clam wearing glasses reads stories of yore,
While the sunken ship's crew forms a conga on the floor.
"Arrr matey!" they cackle, with glee in their wails,
As the starlit sea shimmers, spinning their tales.

With laughter like ripples, they haunt for a night,
In the depths of the ocean, all's merry and bright.
The ghosts dance together, in their watery glow,
Crafting silly legends that only they know.

Haunting Murmurs of an Empty Tide

In the sand, a crab takes a stroll,
Whispers of shells play a distant role.
Ghosts of fish dance in the breeze,
Meanwhile, a seagull has stolen my cheese.

Echoes of laughter, a bucket, a spade,
A mermaid now sells lemonade.
The shore is a stage for a clownish show,
As seaweed artists put on a flow.

Lost flip-flops wade through the foam,
High tides in my backyard, can't be home!
Goldfish in my dreams all wear little hats,
While sharks in suits discuss where they're at.

So bring out your nets, let the frolic begin,
Turn up your toes, let the fun times spin!
With laughter and giggles, the ocean shall roar,
As the jellyfish warm up for a dance on the floor.

The Forgotten Map of the Sea

A map of the ocean, oh what a sight,
X marks the spot, but the 'X' lost its light.
Directions are scribbles from ages ago,
Perhaps it leads to a grinning taco.

Sharks in sunglasses swim with such grace,
While octopuses play in a paper chase.
Forgotten treasures, a rusty old shoe,
A pirate's lost sock, just one, not a crew!

The compass keeps spinning, quite dizzy and wild,
As we sail past sea turtles—a kid's dream beguiled.
Watch out for crabs with their spectral delight,
They argue over who gets the last sea sprite!

A tale of adventure in ocean's embrace,
Where laughter and silliness take center space.
If you find the map, just follow your nose,
To treasures of giggles where the seaweed grows!

Remnants of Lighthouses Lost

The lighthouse flickers in a resigned sigh,
It once warned ships, now it just waves goodbye.
Lanterns gone dim, they tell tall tales,
Of sea monsters chasing fishermen's pails.

A buoy floats by with a mischievous grin,
Riding the waves like it knows it can win.
The cats of the coast hold a council at dusk,
Debating the merits of tuna or musk.

Once proud and bright, now covered in grit,
Pelicans ponder: "Did we take a wrong hit?"
With echoes of laughter, the sea casts a spell,
As barnacles ponder, "Who wears this shell?"

So here in the ruins of light lost at sea,
We toast to the ghosts of buoyancy glee.
In laughter we soar, as the waves join the cheer,
For a lighthouse forgotten has nothing to fear!

Waves That No Longer Call

Once they would crash with a dramatic flair,
Now gentle ripples just whisper and stare.
The ocean's now urging a 'please stay awhile,'
As sea foam gently tickles and beguiles.

Gone are the storms that would dance on the shore,
Replaced with nudging from a clam's gentle snore.
A dolphin once boasted of tricks he could do,
Now sleeps on a buoy wearing bright fuzzy blue.

Where did the surfboards and beach balls all roam?
Are they off on vacation, looking for home?
The gulls now just snicker and wander about,
While jellyfish giggle, "Well, who gives a shout?"

So let's splash and frolic, pretend to be free,
In a world where the ocean both chuckles with glee.
With waves in retreat, oh what shall we call,
This whimsical dance of the waves that can't brawl?

Forgotten Dreams on the Horizon

A dream once sailed on a rubber duck,
It floated away, what a stroke of luck!
Balloons tied to thoughts that never grew,
Like socks in the dryer, they vanished too.

The sun took a nap, the moon wore a frown,
While jellybeans danced in a sugary gown.
Seagulls were laughing, they thought it was neat,
As fish wore sunglasses, swaying to beat.

Shells gossip softly, their stories unsung,
Of crabs in a turret where pranks first were flung.
Oh, the wisdom of waves that once kissed the shore,
They tickle the sands - always craving more.

Yet here in the breeze, the laughter will stay,
With whispers of dreams that just drifted away.
A flip-flop parade mustered up with a cheer,
Here's to the nonsense, bring back the weird!

Waves of Yesterday's Ghosts

Ghosts of the past wear their finest pretzels,
As seaweed wraps round like loving medals.
A pirate's old sock found afloat on a wave,
Tells tales of mishaps, adventures it gave.

The sandcastles tremble, but don't shed a tear,
For crabs are the builders - they hold it all dear.
With shells for the windows and sea foam for roofs,
They throw silly parties where laughter's the proof.

One whispering wave brings a joke from the past,
About clams that ran races - how long did they last?
The punchline submerged, it bubbles and plays,
As bubbles giggle up through the salty spray.

Oh, laughter prevails as the tide fetches fun,
In the land of the lost, where all's come undone.
The marine life oblivious, swims with delight,
They boogie 'neath starfish in the moon's silver light.

The Last Song of the Ocean's Heart

An octopus strummed on a harp made of kelp,
While clownfish chorused, they couldn't help.
The seaweed swayed like it knew all the moves,
As jellyfish twirled, proving they've got grooves.

A crab with a hat, flipped its claws in the air,
Proclaimed all the seas were a reason to share.
With laughter and bubbles, they sang till the dawn,
While sea turtles waltzed on the shimmering lawn.

The gulls joined the band, squawking out their tune,
With laughter and echo, they howled at the moon.
The ocean's heart beats in rhythm so bright,
As the waves play the music under stars' gentle light.

So let's dance alongside with winks and a grin,
To the last song of laughter, where life begins!
Forget all your worries, just flow like the sea,
In this raucous ballet, be wild and be free!

Veils of Seafoam Memories

A seafoam veil drapes on the shore so wide,
Hiding all secrets that snicker and glide.
The starfish held hands with a sulking old log,
As seagulls enjoyed tales beneath the smog.

Blowfish with goggles, they swim, they explore,
While crabs tell old stories nobody could bore.
They giggled and wiggled, spun tales with delight,
Of fish that wore suits at the fancy sea night.

The laughter of whirlpools spins round and round,
As mermaids play tag in the waves they had found.
Oh, the ocean's a ball, with its humor afloat,
Like old socks and sneakers that drifted and wrote.

So raise up a toast to the memories made,
With the jellybean jokes that will never fade.
In veils of the frothy, where dreams love to meet,
Let's fill up our hearts with a laugh and a beat!

The Distant Call of the Unseen

In the sand, a clam digs deep,
While seagulls gossip, secrets to keep.
A crab walks sideways, proud and spry,
Waves crashing softly, oh my, oh my!

The sun slips down, wearing a crown,
Fishy friends swim upside down.
Mermaids laugh, with tails to flaunt,
Jellyfish float like a wobbly taunt.

A treasure chest half-buried in muck,
Filled with rubber ducks—what a luck!
A fisherman's tale with a twist so grand,
"Caught a fish this big!"—a wave of his hand.

So listen close to the frothy cheer,
The ocean's grumble, oh so near.
For in each splash, and each silly squeal,
Lies a story that's wacky, and very real!

Chasing Shadows of the Abyss

There's a ghostly whale with a bowtie style,
Swims through the dark, with a toothy smile.
An octopus knitting, what an odd sight,
Wearing two hats, thinking he's bright!

Crabs in tuxedos dance on the sand,
While shrimp tap their feet, oh isn't it grand?
The deep sea laughs at its own silly plight,
Bubbles of laughter sparkle the night.

A mermaid lost her favorite shoe,
It's now a throne for a clam or two.
With a wave of her hand, she sends a decree,
"Return my shoe, or dance with thee!"

So down we plunge to the sunken floor,
Where antics abound and surprises galore.
For laughter echoes in watery halls,
Chasing shadows, where fun never stalls!

In the Depths of Forgotten Time

Once was a fish with quite a flair,
He wore a hat, my what a pair!
He strutted along with such great pride,
While starfish sang, oh how they tried!

A rusty ship calls, "Who wants to dance?"
With barnacles grooving, they took a chance.
Seashells clapped, and dolphins flew,
In this waltz of the waters, away they flew.

Old treasures laugh at their rusty fate,
"Once we were gold, now check our rate!"
With each wave's crash comes a giggle clear,
A joke from the deep that everyone hears.

So let's dive down to the sights unseen,
Join the strange circus of sea's routine.
For in laughter's embrace, we find our rhymes,
In the depths, we dance through forgotten times!

A World Beneath the Forgetting Sea

Under the waves, where the merfolk play,
A narwhal juggles shells all day.
With every splash, and every spin,
The fish all cheer, "Let's try again!"

The seabed's a stage, with seaweed bows,
Sea cucumbers dancing, oh how it grows!
A slapstick scene with each little pout,
"Don't take my spot!" they scuffle about.

Bubbles rise up, tickling the krill,
Anemones giggle, can't sit still.
As jellyfish float like silly balloons,
The ocean hums funny, playful tunes.

So join in the fun, and splash around,
Where laughter and joy in each wave is found.
For in this world beneath the foam,
Every silly creature has a home!

Waves of the Unremembered Tomorrow

A sailor danced with a bag of chips,
While seagulls plotted their seafood trips.
He traded fish for a shiny shoe,
But it's lost in the depths of ocean blue.

The waves giggle with tales to tell,
Of a crab named Fred who wore a bell.
He leads the parade in a conch shell throne,
While dolphins laugh and steal his bone.

With starfish hats and jellyfish ties,
They throw a party under moonlit skies.
But forgot the drinks, oh what a fuss!
They served up seaweed — who'd want that, thus?

The sunrise breaks, the fun must cease,
A conga line of barnacles, at least!
Tomorrow comes with more fish to fry,
But who will remember? Not this guy!

Isle of Whispers in the Wind

On an isle where whispers tickle the air,
The inhabitants float without a care.
They toast with coconuts, giggling loud,
At the ghostly pirate, who wears a shroud.

A parrot shared jokes, oh what a hoot!
He squawks, 'Why did the crab cross the route?'
To get to the beach where the fries are crisp,
And dance with the mermaids with a groovy lisp.

Their laughter echoes, a soft serenade,
While crabs in tuxedos cut a grand parade.
They moonwalk on sands, in their shiny shoes,
While octopuses serve them seafood stews.

Alas, the tide flows and tickles their toes,
But they don't shy away, oh no, heaven knows!
With a wink and a flip, they splash with glee,
In the isle where the whispers are wild and free!

The Silence Beyond the Breaking Waves

A clam once claimed it held great secrets,
While crabs rolled their eyes, saying 'Just eat it!'
The hush was loud, like a silent scream,
As fish swam by, lost in a dream.

The octopus thought, in a reflective trance,
'What if we danced? Give it a chance!'
But all his arms tangled in seaweed lace,
And the laughter erupted, they fell on their face.

In the silence beyond what the waves could speak,
A whalesong echoed, a bit too bleak.
But starfish chimed in with a quick handstand,
And the sea creatures cheered, 'Now that's just grand!'

With bubbles of joy and splashes of cheer,
They celebrated all the ocean's weirdness here.
Quiet no more, they sang and spun,
For the silence made room for their ocean fun!

Forgotten Shores Beneath the Stars

The sands once whispered of forgotten tales,
Of mermaids knitting their fishy scales.
But a crab built a castle, all out of shells,
And the locals showed up, ringing their bells.

With a flip and a flop, they had a sandball show,
Where the waves cheered loud, 'Give it a go!'
A clam took the stage, with a comedic flair,
While the dolphins rolled in, they laughed in midair.

Stars twinkled brightly, like disco lights,
As they danced in circles, under starry nights.
Forgotten stories of joy and cheer,
Washed ashore on laughter, year after year.

But alas, when dawn broke, the fun would end,
Yet they'd remember tides of joy, my friend.
For beneath those stars, the night was bright,
With forgotten shores and love in sight!

The Stillness of Unwritten Farewells

In a café, the chairs are aligned,
With ghosts of debates left behind.
We sip on our tea, it gets cold,
And stories remain yet untold.

The clock on the wall ticks in a tease,
While we act like we're busy, oh please!
A toast to the friends who won't quit,
But dodged that goodbye — how clever, I admit!

We raise a cup to our missed trains,
To laughter that spills like old refrains.
A wink to the words that won't make the page,
For silence can be the loudest stage.

So here we dwell in this fine café,
Where farewells are soft as a purring cat's play.
In the stillness, we find our escape,
From the scripts of life that we won't reshape.

Swells of Sorrow and Regret

Down by the pier, the fish have a chat,
They gossip 'bout humans, imagine that!
Regret is a tide that won't seem to flee,
As I trip on a crab — what a sight to see!

With each splash, the seagulls are wise,
They steal my chips right before my eyes.
Oh, sorrow's a wave that's all too familiar,
Yet here I laugh as I tighten my chinchilla.

Each net that I cast is a wish or a plan,
But instead, I'm just feeding the seabird clan.
A sailor once brave is now crafting a song,
While the wind winks at me, "You can't get it wrong!"

So let's celebrate all the dreams that we've lost,
Together with seagulls, we dance at the cost.
In this ocean of mishaps, we'll splash and we'll play,
For not all great tales have to end in dismay.

The Embrace of Distant Shores

On distant shores where the sand's a delight,
I find in my pocket a half-eaten bite.
A crab rolls by with its rhythmic beat,
While I try to eat it on a runaway seat.

The ocean whispers tales of old,
Of pirates who ran with treasure untold.
Yet here I am, with flip-flops askew,
Trading fish stories with a gull — who knew?

As the waves laugh loudly, I join in the fun,
My tan lines declare this day is well done.
With sunscreen on my nose like a clowning fool,
I wave at the dolphins who don't think I'm cool.

So let's spin the stories with laughter and mirth,
For on this fine shore lies the laughter of earth.
Distant and close, we find joy in the blend,
Where beaches and buddies embrace 'til the end.

Where the Echoes Fade Away

In valleys where echoes are tossed in the air,
I stumbled on memories that once held great flair.
But now with a grin, I just wave them goodbye,
As echoes turn silly like a well-timed pie.

The mountains chuckle, they know all my woes,
With valleys that giggle as the cool breeze flows.
I trip on my thoughts, and the laughter subsides,
Yet the crickets still chirp, they're sporting their pride.

With each step I take, the past pulls a prank,
Where I think I'm a hero, the hills steal my clank.
So up high and far where the echoes will lay,
I'm lost in the bramble but grin — what a day!

As laughter surrounds where the echoes dissolve,
I find that the memories are puzzles to solve.
In the fade of the twilight, I dance on my way,
For where echoes get quiet, joy learns how to play.

Secrets Entangled in Seaweed

The seaweed laughs with a ticklish glee,
Whispers of jellyfish dancing with me.
Lost in the murky, a crab plays the fool,
While starfish ponder if they've broken a rule.

An oyster named Gary tells tales of the deep,
Of treasures and trinkets he's sworn to keep.
But when it gets tricky, he'll slip on a shell,
And blame it on currents that tug at him well.

Barnacles gossip, oh what a crew,
About the fish that once wore a shoe.
But spotted a whale, they chuckle with zest,
"We like our hard shells; the soft ones can rest!"

So gather the sea critters, hear their delight,
In underwater chaos, the world feels just right.
With secrets entangled in laughter and mirth,
The ocean is home, and it's filled with their worth.

Ghost Stories Across the Waters

The seagulls squawk, "Beware of the gray!",
It's the ghost of a pirate who ran out of pay.
He roams wooden docks with a bottle in hand,
Telling tales of treasure and ships made of sand.

A mermaid once waved, "Come swim with the dead!",
But the octopus chuckled and shook his big head.
"Those stories are silly, they're fish tales at best,
We'll stick to our reefs, where we feel quite blessed!"

In foggy old ports, the whispers abide,
Of a phantom clam that refuses to hide.
He boasts of his pearls but never lets go,
Leaving fishermen laughing, that clam steals the show!

So raise up a glass of the salty sea brew,
To ghostly fish tales that are funny but true.
They swim through the currents, just like you and me,
In watery realms where the laughter runs free.

The Abyss of Unanswered Questions

What swims in the depths? A lost shoe or two,
Do fishes need glasses, or what do they view?
The bubbles keep popping, a riddle in foam,
Are they laughing at sailors who never come home?

Do turtles tell secrets when out on a stroll?
Like "Why do the clams keep on guarding their gold?"
While octopuses plot with eight arms intertwined,
They roll on the sea floor, perplexed and confined.

The crabs carry wisdom in their pinchers, so sly,
As they ponder hard questions like "Why does fish fly?"
They dig deep in sand, where their answers must rest,
But the wit of a whale then puts them to test.

With glee in the currents, confusion can reign,
As laughter bubbles up in a mysterious chain.
In the abyss, we ponder with gills laboring hard,
But in this fancy deep, it's just all a card.

Memoirs Adrift in the Ocean's Breath

An old sea sponge writes with a quill made of shell,
Of fishy adventures and mishaps to tell.
The tales of the wave that knocked over the boat,
Or the time that a dolphin wore an old coat!

Each paragraph bursts with a splash and a flip,
Of crabs who collided and fell from their grip.
The shrimp dance the jig on the warm sandy floor,
While the currents collect all the swabbies' folklore.

In memoirs of bubbles, the laughter does rise,
As the old sea turtle recalls every prize.
Like the time he mistook a big rock for a friend,
And ended up stuck 'til it was the day's end.

So gather around, hear the ocean's sweet sighs,
Of memoirs adrift under bright, twinkling skies.
With tales of the deep that'll tickle your heart,
In this funny old sea, we all play a part.

www.ingramcontent.com/pod-product-compliance
Lightning Source LLC
Chambersburg PA
CBHW062113280426
43661CB00086B/588